WHO, WHAT, WHY?

WHAT

THE TABERNACLE?

CF4·K

DANIKA COOLEY

10 9 8 7 6 5 4 3 2 1
Copyright © Danika Cooley 2024
Paperback ISBN: 978-1-5271-1175-2
ebook ISBN: 978-1-5271-1240-7

Published by
Christian Focus Publications,
Geanies House, Fearn, Tain, Ross-shire,
IV20 1TW, Scotland, U.K.
www.christianfocus.com
email: info@christianfocus.com

Printed and bound by Bell and Bain, Glasgow

MIX
Paper | Supporting
responsible forestry
FSC® C007785

Cover design by Catriona Mackenzie
Illustrations by Martyn Smith

TABLE OF CONTENTS

Dedication

To the Reader (That's you!)
May you follow Jesus,
and may God dwell with you.

THE AUTHOR

Danika Cooley and her husband, Ed, are committed to leading their children to live for the glory of God. Danika has a passion for equipping parents to teach the Bible and Christian history to their kids. She is the author of *Help Your Kids Learn and Love the Bible, When Lightning Struck!: The Story of Martin Luther, Bible Investigators: Creation, Wonderfully Made: God's Story of Life from Conception to Birth*, and the *Who, What, Why?* Series about the history of our faith. Danika's three year Bible survey curriculum, Bible Road Trip™, is used by families around the world. Weekly, she encourages tens of thousands of parents to intentionally raise biblically literate children. Danika is a homeschool mother of four with a Bachelor of Arts degree from the University of Washington. Find her at ThinkingKidsBlog.org.

A PEOPLE
FOR GOD

In the beginning, before there were lakes with fish, mountains with trees, or deserts full of sand, there was God. Our God, Yahweh—whose name means I AM WHO I AM—has always been. Yahweh is. Yahweh always will be.

Now, there is only one God, Yahweh. But it is a great mystery and amazing truth that our God is three Persons in one God. There is God the Father, God the Son—who is Jesus, and God the Holy Spirit.

In the beginning, after God created the earth, he made a man named Adam and a woman named Eve. God also created marriage as a gift for a man and a woman to share together, and Adam took Eve as his wife. In the Garden of Eden, their home, God placed many wonderful trees with fruit for Adam and Eve to eat, but he told Adam, "Of the tree of the knowledge of good and evil you shall not eat, for in the day that you eat of it you shall surely die."

Though God is the creator of heaven and earth, he came down to walk with his people. On the day Adam and Eve ate the forbidden fruit of the tree of the knowledge of good and evil, they hid because they had sinned. To sin is to rebel against God—to break his rules. And, that's just what they had done. Sin brought with it a curse and death entered creation. God placed a cherubim—a type of angel—with a sword at the gate to the garden. God no longer physically walked with his people.

The book of Genesis in the Bible tells the story of just how sinful God's people can be. Yet, throughout the history of human rebellion, God has been with individuals who feared and honored him. God was

with Noah. God was with Abraham. God was with Isaac, Jacob, and Joseph. And, God had a great plan to reunite forever with his people long before Adam and Eve ever sinned.

In the days of God's prophet, Moses, the Israelites—descendants of Abraham, Isaac, and Jacob—lived in the land of Egypt as slaves to an evil Pharaoh who rebelled against God. Pharaoh did not even believe Yahweh existed. So, God brought his chosen people, the Israelites, out of Egypt using miracles to show that he, alone, is the Lord God, Yahweh. God was with Moses and the Israelites in a pillar of cloud by day and a pillar of fire at night.

Now, God's people had been rebelling, too, worshiping the fake gods of Egypt just as Pharaoh did. Some Israelites worshiped God, but not the way God wants to be worshiped. So, while his people camped in the wilderness at the base of Mount Sinai, God gave Moses rules to teach his people how to love him and how to love each other. God also gave Moses instructions for how to build a fabulous tabernacle—a moveable temple for the Lord. That way, the Israelites would know how to serve and worship God his way, in reverence and awe.

This tabernacle was erected exactly one year after God brought the Israelites out of slavery in Egypt. God's pillar of cloud settled on the tabernacle, and God's glory filled it. He was with his people. Every night, his glory burned like a fire in the tabernacle. The tabernacle reminded the people of Israel that our sin separates us from God, that he made a way for us to approach him, and that our great God should be worshiped his way.

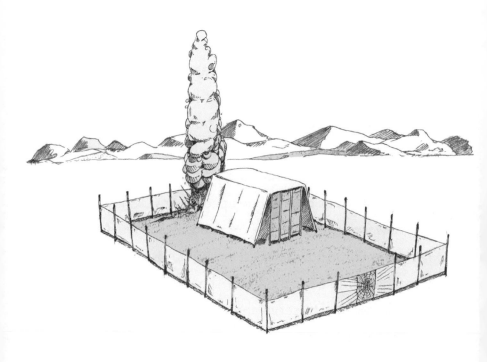

Several hundred years passed after God brought the Israelites into the Promised Land. Then, King Solomon built the temple—a more permanent tabernacle—in Jerusalem. God dwelled there among his people.

Much later, Jesus—who is God the Son, and the Son of God—was born on earth. The apostle John wrote in John 1:14: "And the Word became flesh and dwelt among us, and we have seen his glory, glory as of the only Son from the Father, full of grace and truth." Jesus is the living Word of God. He dwelt among us, teaching us to love God, to love each other, and to worship God in God's own way.

Jesus lived a perfect, sinless life before he took the punishment for the sin of every person who believes in Jesus. Then, three days after Jesus was crucified, he was raised from the dead. After appearing alive to many witnesses, Jesus ascended to heaven. He will return again one day to gather his people to live with him forever.

Throughout time, the great I AM has dwelled with his people. Today, God is still with us. God the Holy Spirit dwells in the heart of each person who believes in Jesus and repents of—turns from—their sin.

The tabernacle was a wonderful picture God gave his people to help them understand who God is, why we need a Savior, and how we can worship God rightly. Each aspect of the tabernacle points to Jesus in some way.

THE STAIN OF SIN

Sinning is like dumping black ink into the washing machine. Nothing comes out clean. Instead, everything is stained.

Romans 6:23 says: "For the wages of sin is death, but the free gift of God is eternal life in Christ Jesus our Lord." You see, every one of us has sinned. We are stained by our rebellion against God. The punishment for our rebellion is eternal death—separation from God forever.

But, our great God has a plan for salvation. Hebrews 9:22b says, "Without the shedding of blood there is no forgiveness of sins." Jesus Christ shed his own blood for us so we can be forgiven. With the stain of our rebellion gone, we can live forever with the one true God, Yahweh.

WORSHIP IN
THE DESERT

After God led the Israelites out of Egypt, they camped in the wilderness at Mount Sinai, the mountain of God. Yahweh called Moses up the mountain to receive laws. While Moses was on Mount Sinai, God said to him: "Let them make me a sanctuary, that I may dwell in their midst. Exactly as I show you concerning the pattern of the tabernacle, and of all its furniture, so you shall make it" (Exodus 25:8-9). So, Moses and the Israelites followed all of God's instructions in making the tabernacle.

Our God is holy—he is perfect, good, and exalted. God is set apart from his creation. So, our worship of God must also be holy. Because our God is a God of order, our worship of him must also be ordered.

Today, God's commands for worship in the Old Testament may seem strange, and not at all like the way we worship God today. After all, Old Testament worship was bloody. Remember, the wages of sin is death. That means that all sin must be paid for with the blood of sacrifice. So, the Old Testament believers repented of their sin and turned to God by sacrificing an animal. Instead of a worshiper dying for their sin, God accepted the blood of a perfect animal that had no blemish—the best goat, lamb, bull, ram, or dove the worshiper had to offer.

God's tabernacle was designed to be portable, so it could be broken down and moved to a new campsite whenever the cloudy pillar of God's glory lifted from the tabernacle and moved ahead. The tribe of Levi— one of the twelve tribes of Israel—was responsible for the worship of God in the tabernacle. They also moved and set up the tabernacle in a new location when the pillar of cloud and fire stopped. God led his people and dwelled with them as they moved through the desert wilderness on their way to the Promised Land.

The tabernacle had an outer courtyard where animals were sacrificed and priests washed their hands and feet to show themselves ceremonially clean. The tabernacle building itself was divided into two separate rooms—the Holy Place and the Most Holy Place. There were several ways the priests worshiped God in the Holy Place: using a lampstand, an altar of incense, and a table for the bread of presence.

Remember that God was with his people in the desert. The Most Holy Place was God's throne room here on earth. In that room sat the ark of the covenant with the mercy seat on top. There, God's presence dwelled when the cloud descended on the tabernacle.

Now, God does not really live in a cloud. God is actually everywhere all the time. And, though God dwells—or lives—with us, he is not at all confined to one place or even one time in history. But, he helped us understand that he is with us by showing his glory through his presence in the pillar of cloud and fire.

When the people killed an innocent animal to pay for their sin, it helped them understand that their sin was a serious offense against our good God. The payment for sin is always painful and sad. Chapter 10 in the book of Hebrews tells us that it is truly impossible for the blood of bulls and goats to take away our sins. That's why the worshipers in the Old Testament had to sacrifice animals over and over again. They were under the Old Covenant, which was God's legal treaty with his people before Jesus was born. The sacrifices were a reminder of sin's stain, but the animal blood did not offer permanent forgiveness.

However, when Jesus died on the cross for us, God created a New Covenant—a new treaty—with his people. God established a new way for us to repent of our sin and be forgiven, once and for all. You see, Jesus took the sin of every believer upon himself and died in their place. Then, he sat down at the right hand of our Father God in the true, heavenly throne room of Yahweh. God has written his law on the hearts and minds of those who trust in him. Because of the blood of Jesus, we can approach God in prayer and in worship, knowing that we are forgiven and clean from the stain of sin.

Now, sometimes people invent fantastic meanings for each of the tabernacle materials. But, it's important to read God's Word—Scripture—in the light of Scripture. The book of Hebrews tells us how to interpret the symbolism behind aspects of God's portable temple. Jesus helped us understand more about himself in the book of John.

While we can look for clues in history, we must be careful not to add meaning to God's Word. We must look to what God himself tells us in the Bible. Careful Bible detectives—like you—study God's Word by examining other passages in Scripture. This helps us understand what God is saying to us. We learn more about how the tabernacle points to Jesus by reading Hebrews 8-10 alongside Exodus 25-40, parts of the Gospel of John, and the book of Leviticus—which is God's handbook to the priests.

A SHADOW OF THE TRUTH

Hebrews 9:23-24 tells us the tabernacle and the offerings are "copies of the heavenly things." Jesus' heavenly sacrifice, though, is better: "For Christ has entered, not into holy places made with hands, which are copies of the true things, but into heaven itself, now to appear in the presence of God on our behalf."

God often gives us word pictures and stories to help us better understand heavenly truths. The tabernacle is a type, also called a figure or shadow, of heavenly truths. It points to Jesus and to God's plan for salvation. Hebrews 10:1 tells us the law is just a shadow of reality.

The law can never make us perfect through sacrifices offered repeatedly. Jesus, though, can remove the stain of our sin.

PEOPLE GIVING
TO YAHWEH

Do you wonder how God's people, just freed from slavery, built a spectacular tabernacle in the wilderness? There were no hardware stores to stop at or contractors to call up, after all. Well, God has a plan for everything. He had a plan for the building of the tabernacle!

Four hundred and thirty years before God brought his people out of slavery in Egypt, he made a promise to the Israelite patriarch, Abraham. God promised Abraham that his offspring would live in a land that was not theirs. There, they would suffer and work as servants. Then, 400 years later, God would judge the enslaving nation and bring his people out with many possessions. Finally, he would give them the land of Canaan as their own homeland.

So, God brought judgment on Egypt through a series of plagues. Then, just before the first Passover, when the firstborn son of every household in Egypt died in one night, God told Moses to send the people of Israel to ask their Egyptian neighbors for silver and gold jewelry. God gave the people favor with the Egyptians, and Moses, too, was regarded as an important man in Egypt. That's how God's people came out of Egypt with all kinds of brass, gold, silver, dyed yarns, leather, and even gemstones.

Now, three months later, when Moses went up Mount Sinai to meet with God, the Lord told him to ask the Israelites for a contribution. The people of God were each to give materials for the tabernacle. So, Moses gathered everyone and said, "If you have a generous heart, the Lord has commanded you to bring

what is needed for the tabernacle." That's exactly what the people did. They made piles and piles of materials for God's portable temple.

Those who loved God joyfully brought gold jewelry. They took the armbands off their arms and dropped them on the pile. By the time the people had finished, there was over three thousand pounds of gold—more than a car weighs. The Israelites piled up about seven thousand pounds of bronze—nearly as much as a pickup truck!

Next, the Lord had the people pay a tax, a half shekel for each man over the age of twenty. Over six hundred and three thousand men contributed. God's men gave so much silver, that it all weighed about as much as a large motorhome—twelve thousand pounds.

That wasn't all. The Israelites brought even more gifts for God's tabernacle. They made piles of blue yarn, purple yarn, and scarlet yarn. There was flax to weave into linen, too. Piles of goat hair stood next to stacks of tanned ram skins, which towered over goat skins. Acacia wood was stacked in rows. The people lined up jars and jars of oil from olives they beat by hand. They brought jars of spices, too. The leaders of the people—who had the best stuff—brought precious gemstones and black onyx stone for the special outfit the High Priest would wear.

The people brought so many gifts for the tabernacle that the men in charge of the construction came to Moses. "Moses!" they cried, "The people are bringing too much for the tabernacle. We have more than enough for the work that the Lord has commanded we do."

So, Moses sent word throughout the camp, "Don't give any more! We have enough contributions to finish the tabernacle!"

It must have been a magnificent sight, more than two million Israelites lining up to give their treasures to the Lord. God had been generous with the Israelites. He brought them out of slavery, cared for them in the wilderness, and moved the hearts of the Egyptians to load them down with riches. In return, the people of God gave some of their wonderful belongings right back to God.

That is how we should live, too. You see, nothing we have truly belongs to us. Everything you own is a gift—a blessing—from God. You are a caretaker for your blessings, and the Lord wants you to share.

In 2 Corinthians 9:6-8, the apostle Paul wrote to the church at Corinth, "The point is this: whoever sows sparingly will also reap sparingly, and whoever sows bountifully will also reap bountifully. Each one must give as he has decided in his heart, not reluctantly or under compulsion, for God loves a cheerful giver. And God is able to make all grace abound to you, so that having all sufficiency in all things at all times, you may abound in every good work."

You see, God gives to us all sorts of good things. We are grateful to God, and we cheerfully give to others. God gives us what we need—and enough to share. Verses 11-14 tell us that the Lord gives us enough to be generous. That way, we will give God thanks. The whole point is that we overflow with thanksgiving. When we give to others who are in need, they glorify God, and they will pray for you.

FIVE OFFERINGS

The burnt offering showed that a person was dedicated to God. Blood was sprinkled on the altar, and the lamb was completely burned.

A sin offering was for accidental sins, while a guilt offering was for intentional sins against others. Very poor people could bring two pigeons or doves. A priest sacrificed a bull, a ruler sacrificed a male goat, and common people sacrificed a female lamb. Then, the priest ate the cooked meat.

The fellowship—or peace—offering gave thanks to God. Part of the animal went to the priest, and the worshiper ate the rest in a joyful feast with guests.

Worshipers thanked God with a grain offering of roasted grain, flour, or unleavened cake. Some was crumbled at the altar while the priests ate the rest.

THE OUTER
COURTYARD

God's tabernacle must have been an amazing sight, with God dwelling right in the middle of his people. You see, God had Moses situate the tabernacle right in the middle of camp, with the Israelite tribes camped around it in an orderly manner, three tribes on each side. Then, the priestly tribe of the Levites camped in between the people and the portable temple.

The golden tabernacle, also called the tent of meeting, was surrounded by a white fence made of linen. The linen would have stood out spectacularly against the dry wilderness terrain, catching the attention of neighboring tribes. The gate to the tabernacle was woven into a blue, purple, and scarlet tapestry. The gate always faced east, with the tent of meeting against the back fence. A large courtyard stretched in front.

The linen fence curtains were linked by silver hooks to acacia wood posts that were wrapped in silver, with gleaming silver caps on top. The cross bars were silver, too. The posts sat in bronze bases on the wilderness soil. The whole fence was about one quarter the size of a football field, and seven and a half feet high.

Now, every Israelite child rose from bed in the morning and went out to help their parents gather manna—the bread God sent from heaven to feed his people. Had you been there, you would have looked up at the pure white fence with the gleaming silver post caps and the golden tabernacle towering nearly twice as tall as the fencing. And you would have marveled as you saw the glory of God rise in a pillar of cloud.

In the courtyard, smoke billowed upward from the morning sacrifices. Lambs were bleating, bulls were bellowing, and golden utensils for the altar were clanking. The smell of cooking meat and burning incense filled the air while worshipers lined up outside the gate with their finest goats and doves, waiting for their turn to sacrifice to the Lord. Outside the tabernacle, the priests inspected animals, then blessed the people.

You would have removed your shoes and entered the courtyard through the gate. There, you would come face-to-face with the bronze altar. Made of acacia wood, covered in bronze, with a brass horn on each corner, the altar was seven and a half feet long on each side with poles to carry it. Your sacrifice would have been tied to one of the horns and placed on the brass grate inside the hollow altar.

Animals died for the sins of the worshiper, and it was important that each person remember the wages of their sin is death. So, you would have placed your

hands on your lamb's head. Maybe you would pray, remembering out loud before God that your sin is worthy of death. Then, you would ask God to transfer your sin to the innocent lamb. Finally, the lamb would be sacrificed. The priest would catch the blood in a bowl, sprinkling it around the altar, then pouring the excess out at the base of the altar.

Around the courtyard, bustling priests would be shoveling ash from under the altar, stocking it with more wood to create coal, which was used to fill the censers. Other priests would prod and arrange

sacrifices on the altar, or fill their censers with burning coals to carry into the Holy Place. If you looked toward the fifteen-foot tall golden tabernacle, you would see a large, bronze washbasin filled with gleaming water.

The washbasin would be shining like a mirror in the sun. Actually, it was made of mirrors. The women who stood at the gate of the tabernacle to pray and worship had donated the polished bronze mirrors they used to examine their hair and faces. Those mirrors were pounded and polished into the washbasin, then the whole thing was placed on feet of brass. Priests preparing to enter the tent of meeting would wash their hands and feet in order to be ceremonially clean.

To come near to God we, too, must be purified. Sin is like an ugly stain on our hearts which we cannot rinse clean with water. The blood of Jesus, though, can wash our hearts so they are spotless of sin. Hebrews 10:22 says, "Let us draw near with a true heart in full assurance of faith, with our hearts sprinkled clean from an evil conscience and our bodies washed with pure water." The water in this verse refers to the blood of Jesus. His sacrifice is the only way for us to be purified after our rebellion toward God.

In the courtyard of the tabernacle, worshipers learned that their sin was worthy of death. God made a way for a substitute—a lamb—to die in the worshiper's place. Today, we understand that God was using the tabernacle to prepare the hearts of his people to understand Jesus better. You see, Jesus is our sacrificial Lamb of God, who died in our place.

Hebrews 9:11-14 tells us there is a greater and more perfect tent—God's heavenly throne room. Jesus entered the holy places in heaven and he secured for us an eternal salvation. If you look to Jesus for salvation, his blood cleans your conscience—and your heart—so that you can enter the presence of our holy God.

THE PASSOVER AND THE FEAST

God's feasts were a time for his people to rest, give thanks, repent, and read Scripture together.

The Feast of Unleavened Bread lasted seven days each year. On the first night, Passover, each Israelite family painted the blood of a spotless lamb on the doorframe of their house. They ate lamb, unleavened

bread, and bitter herbs, remembering the night God led his people out of slavery in Egypt. God passed over every house covered by the blood of the sacrificial lamb, but the oldest son of every Egyptian family died.

When Jesus, our Passover Lamb, was crucified, his blood covered the sins of believers. Today, we remember his sacrifice through the celebration of the Lord's Supper, or Communion.

ARTISTS
GIFTED BY GOD

God gave Moses detailed blueprints for his tabernacle. Then, God called the people to contribute everything their hearts told them to give. God also provided a way for the tabernacle to be built solidly and beautifully, so it was a marvel to behold.

Moses called the people together, saying, "God has called Bezalel, son of Uri, son of Hur, of the tribe of Judah!" Perhaps Moses had Bezalel stood beside him. "God has filled Bezalel with the Holy Spirit of God. The Spirit of God has given Bezalel skill, intelligence, knowledge, and all craftsmanship."

You see, the Lord gave Bezalel the ability to create beautiful artistic designs. Not only that, Bezalel was an artist with gold, silver, and bronze. Those metals must be melted and poured, hammered, or carved into the right shapes. Bezalel could do even more—carving wood, cutting gemstones, and anything else he needed to do as a craftsman.

Then Moses announced, "God inspired Bezalel to teach. Oholiab, son of Ahisamach, of the tribe of Dan is gifted, too." Now, perhaps, Oholiab nodded to Bezalel. They were going to work together, teaching their skills to others.

While the Holy Spirit gifted both Bezalel and Oholiab with special ability as engravers, designers, embroiderers, and weavers, the work was too much for just two men. The tabernacle was constructed in just seven months, and was erected just under a

year after God brought his people out of Egypt. So, Bezalel and Oholiab needed help. God had Moses call every craftsman that the Lord had gifted with skill to volunteer. The Holy Spirit moved their hearts to do the work, they grabbed their tools and came forward to help.

There were skilled women, too, who volunteered to spin wool into blue, purple, and scarlet yarns. They spun flax into finely twined linen. As the hearts of the women were turned toward glorifying God, they also skillfully spun piles of goat's hair into yarn.

God's gifted craftspeople, artists, and weavers worked side-by-side for seven months, creating the moveable temple in which God would dwell in their midst. They understood that the tabernacle would provide everything they needed to serve the Lord. And, each one of the artists was gifted by God to serve him, then called to glorify God through their service.

The craftsmen made the fencing of the tabernacle with its silver posts, hooks, and caps. Bronze bases held the silver posts steady. For the curtains, the craftsmen used fine, twined linen, with blue, purple, and scarlet gates opening into the courtyard. They made a second blue, purple, and scarlet linen gate to lead into the Holy Place. A third blue, purple, and scarlet curtain led into the Most Holy Place, with cherubim embroidered into the veil. Cherubim were also embroidered into the roof of the tabernacle.

The people would have learned to create the finest linen in the known world during their time in Egypt, where tall flax grew in fields along the Nile river. Each piece of flax was as wide as a milkshake straw. The people cut the flax down by the roots, then dried the straws out in the sun. Next, they pounded the flax over and over again until they could pull out long, fine fibers to weave into thread, then into linen.

The blue thread was likely dyed with the crushed shells of a sea snail found in the Mediterranean Sea. The Israelites had lived in Goshen, Egypt, where the Nile flows into the Mediterranean. Crushing one hundred and fifty thousand shells made just one ounce of blue dye—it was very valuable, indeed. The scarlet dye could be made from the larva of a scale insect that lived on trees. Perhaps the purple color came from mixing the red and blue dyes together. In the days of the Bible, creating beautiful purple linen was expensive because it required a lot of work from incredibly skilled people. So, only royalty wore purple robes. It is fitting that the temple for the King of the Universe used purple linen.

The tabernacle building itself was made from acacia wood boards covered with gold, then fitted into silver frames on three sides. Acacia trees grow as tall as a two-story house, and perhaps as wide as you are tall. The wood grows in dry places, such as the wilderness of Sinai. Because the wood is so hard, insects don't eat it and weather doesn't ruin it. It was perfect for the tabernacle building.

Building the tabernacle required the work of many skilled artists. After God gifted his people to serve him, he moved their hearts to serve with joy. Today, we also must work for our God with joy, knowing that God the Holy Spirit has given each believer gifts to serve him in different ways. Colossians 3:23-24 says, "Whatever you do, work heartily, as for the Lord and not for men, knowing that from the Lord you will receive the inheritance as your reward. You are serving the Lord Christ."

THE FEAST OF FIRSTFRUITS

This feast occurred on the third day of the Feast of Unleavened Bread, before the spring barley harvest. On the third day after the Passover Feast, families took their bundle—the firstfruits harvested from the field—to the tabernacle or temple where the priest waved it before God. It was a way to thank God for his gift of the harvest.

One day, Christians will be raised from the dead to live with God forever. Jesus is the firstfruits of believers who have died. Just as an apple tree produces the first apple, then a whole harvest of apples, Jesus was the first raised from the dead in a forever body so that a harvest of believers will one day also be raised from the dead to live eternally. Today, we celebrate Resurrection Sunday, remembering God's promise of eternal life for every believer.

THE HOLY
PLACE

Nobody could enter the tabernacle behind the bronze washbasin unless, they were a Levite, from the specific line of Aaron. Aaron, his sons, and, later, his grandsons entered the Holy Place to behold a spectacular sight.

The Holy Place was fifteen feet wide and thirty feet long, with four coverings which formed the roof. When the priests walked into the windowless room, seven oil lamps burned from a tall, gold lampstand, lighting the gold walls and silver bases. The priests stood in the flickering light beneath a ceiling filled with the wings of cherubim. The veil into the Most Holy Place matched the ceiling in splendor and design.

Above the cherubim-covered ceiling was a second covering made of spun goat's hair. On top of that was laid a covering of tanned ram's skin leather. The outer layer consisted of tahash skins. Bible scholars have trouble translating the Hebrew word, *tahash*, into English, so some translations say badger or goat skins. While the outer covering could have been made of dolphin skins, it was most likely created from the skin of the dugong—a type of sea cow which swam in the Mediterranean Sea. Waterproof dugong skin would have protected the inside of the tabernacle from the weather.

The Holy Place contained three pieces of furniture, each designed for the worship of God, and to point to Jesus. Bezalel beat the lampstand from a seventy-five-pound block of gold into a spectacular sort of almond tree. The main branch of the lampstand had

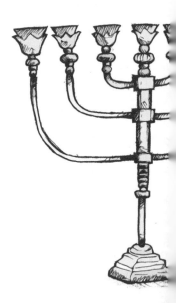

six branches extending on each side. On top of each of the seven branches, an oil lamp resembled an almond blossom just before it blooms. Along the branches, other carved almond blossoms looked ready to open. It was quite beautiful, standing nearly as tall as the priest tending to it.

Jesus was teaching in the temple in Jerusalem during the Feast of Tabernacles when he said, in John 8:12, "I am the light of the world. Whoever follows me will not walk in darkness, but will have the light of life."

When we follow Jesus, we do not walk in the darkness of sin, but in the light of God. Jesus also said that we are the light of the world. That makes sense, doesn't it? God is light, and God the Holy Spirit lives in each believer. If you love and follow Jesus, you are like a bright light to those who need to learn about God's great plan for salvation.

On the right side of the room as the priest entered, across from the lampstand, stood the table of the bread of the presence made of acacia wood covered with gold. Like the altar in the courtyard, it had rings on each corner with poles so the priests could easily move it. The table itself was three feet long, one and a half feet wide, and two and a

quarter feet high. Gold plates held twelve loaves of bread. There were gold pitchers, too, for daily drink offerings. The wine was poured on the ground by the altar.

Jesus was teaching when he said in John 6:48-51, "I am the bread of life. Your fathers ate the manna in the wilderness, and they died. This is the bread that comes down from heaven, so that one may eat of it and not die. I am the living bread that came down from heaven. If anyone eats of this bread, he will live forever. And the bread that I will give for the life of the world is my flesh." Now, Jesus did not mean that people would literally eat his body. Instead, he meant that anyone who believes in him as God the Son and trusts him for salvation will be saved from sin for all eternity. Just like food sustains your life, Jesus gives eternal life to all who follow him.

Right in front of the veil into the Most Holy Place stood the altar of incense. The altar was also made of acacia wood overlaid in gold. It was small, just a foot and a half on each side, and three feet tall, with a gold crown along the top. Priests burned a specific mixture of incense on the altar. The incense included stacte, which was probably a sweet gum from the flowering styrax plant. Frankincense is the white gum of the boswellia tree. Onycha, the shell of a mollusk, was ground up and mixed with stacte, frankincense, and galbanum, a bitter shrub sap. God instructed the priests that only this mixture of spices could be used on the incense altar, and no meat, drink, or strange—unholy—fire was to be offered.

God's Word calls our prayers incense before God. In John 17:9, Jesus told God the Father that he is praying for his people. Hebrews 7:25 tells us that Jesus, our forever Priest, "is able to save to the uttermost those who draw near to God through him, since he always lives to make intercession for them." If you have been cleansed of the stain of sin by Jesus' sacrifice, then he is always praying for you. This is a special incense that pleases God.

THE FEAST OF WEEKS

After the Feast of Firstfruits, the people counted fifty days until the Feast of Weeks. Families traveled to Jerusalem during the wheat harvest with two loaves of bread to be waved before God in the tabernacle.

During the Feast of Weeks, fifty days after Jesus' Resurrection, the disciples heard a sound like wind and saw something like flames come to rest on each of them. They began speaking in the languages of Jews who had traveled from other countries for the feast. Peter explained to the Jewish visitors that Jesus was raised from the dead and had ascended to heaven to sit with God the Father. About three thousand people became Christians that day. Pentecost—which means fifty in Greek—is the day the Holy Spirit came to live in believers.

PRIESTS TO
THE LORD

One of Jacob's sons, Joseph, was sold into slavery by his brothers. He ended up in an Egyptian prison but eventually became second-in-command to Pharaoh. During the famine Joseph's brothers and their families moved to Egypt. However, as the years passed, new Pharaohs oppressed and enslaved the Israelites.

Now, Jacob's third son, Levi, had three sons of his own: Gershon, Kohath, and Merari. At Mount Sinai, God called Levi's descendants—the Levites—to be the priests of Israel, in charge of the worship of God. God gave each family within the Levite tribe a different task to perform.

The Gershonites cared for and moved all the hangings, except for the veil for the Most Holy Place. The tabernacle coverings, two other gates, and linen fencing were all packed carefully in two wagons pulled by four oxen. The Kohathites were responsible for the veil and all the furniture—the altar, washbasin, bread table, lampstand, incense altar, and the ark of the covenant with the mercy seat. Each furniture piece was moved using poles. The Merarites cared for the tabernacle boards, bars, pillars, sockets, and bases—the framework of the fencing and building.

Nine thousand and six hundred men in the Levite tribe worked for three hours to take the tabernacle apart and have it ready to move. These Levites ensured that the bread for the altar was baked. They played music and sang hymns before the Lord. And, they kept the tabernacle ready for the worship of God, ensuring wine, grain, animals, and wood were available for the priests.

Amram, the father of Moses and his siblings, Aaron and Miriam, was descended from Kohath, a son of Levi. God called Aaron to be his High Priest. Only the High Priest was allowed to enter the Most Holy Place each year. This special day was called the Day of Atonement. It was when sacrifices were offered to atone for sins—to reconcile the people with God. That is what atonement means.

Aaron's sons, Nadab, Abihu, Eleazar, and Ithamar, worked as priests. They kept the golden lampstand burning, offered incense, and stocked the altar with bread in the Holy Place. Only priests in the line of

Aaron were allowed to serve in the Holy Place, or to become the next High Priest.

God gave Moses specific instructions for every aspect of worship, including the clothing the priests wore. Aaron and his sons each wore a white linen turban and a coat with a sash embroidered with blue, purple, and scarlet yarns. The High Priest's turban had

a special gold plate that said "Holy to the Lord," which means "Dedicated to Yahweh."

Now, Aaron, the High Priest, wore a blue robe over the top of his coat. Along the hem of the robe were blue, purple, and scarlet pomegranates, with bells between each one. A special vest or apron—called an ephod—was made of linen woven with thin gold sheets and with blue, purple and scarlet yarn. The ephod was tied with a sash, and at each shoulder sat an onyx stone with the names of God's tribes inscribed, six tribes on each shoulder.

The High Priest also wore a special gold breast plate with twelve stones, each engraved with the name of one of the tribes of Israel. Joseph and the Levites were not included. Instead, the names of Joseph's two sons, Manasseh and Ephraim, were inscribed on the stones. This is because the priestly Levite tribe was considered

holy to God, and Joseph's sons each received a special inheritance as a half-tribe.

Worshiping God in our own way, without fear and honor for his holy character, can have dire consequences. Aaron's sons, Nadab and Abihu, dishonored God with disordered worship. They offered incense with unauthorized fire to God. Immediately, fire from the Lord burned them up. While this was a hard punishment, the priests had worshiped God in their own way. Their act of rebellion was immediately

dealt with by God himself. This shows how serious the proper worship of our holy God is.

Today, we do not worship God through priests entering the Holy Place or Most Holy Place. Instead, Jesus is our tabernacle, dwelling with us. He is our Lamb of God, the Light of the World, and the Bread of Life. Jesus prays for us—he is our Mediator, and he is our great High Priest.

Hebrews 7:26-27 says, "For it was indeed fitting that we should have such a high priest, holy, innocent, unstained, separated from sinners, and exalted above the heavens. He has no need, like those high priests, to offer sacrifices daily, first for his own sins and then for those of the people, since he did this once for all when he offered up himself." Jesus took the sins of believers on himself and offered himself as a sacrifice to cover our sins.

Next, Hebrews 8:1-2 says, "Now the point in what we are saying is this: we have such a high priest, one who is seated at the right hand of the throne of the Majesty in heaven, a minister in the holy places, in the true tent that the Lord set up, not man." Jesus died for us, and now he sits in the true, heavenly Most Holy Place, as our High Priest forever.

THE FEAST OF TRUMPETS

In Autumn, the people of Israel celebrated a day of rest and repentance with sacrifices and trumpet blasts. To repent is to turn away from sin and turn toward God. We must acknowledge we have rebelled against God, then turn to follow God rather than our own evil desires.

The Bible tells us that Jesus will return to gather his people and judge unbelievers. On that day, there will be a great trumpet blast. In 2 Corinthians 6:2b, the apostle Paul writes, "Behold, now is the day of salvation." One day, it will be too late to repent, and the trumpet will sound. Have you talked to a Christian adult about what it means to repent and follow Jesus?

THE MOST
HOLY PLACE

One day each year, the High Priest entered the Most Holy Place, a room fifteen feet wide and long, through a heavy veil embroidered with cherubim. Holding an incense censer, the High Priest approached the earthly throne of God with the utmost respect and honor. In John 10:7-9, Jesus says that he is the Door. Those who enter by him are saved. Then, in John 14:6, Jesus tells the apostle Thomas, "I am the way, and the truth, and the life. No one comes to the Father except through me." Just as the only way to the tabernacle throne room was through the veil, the only way to salvation is through God's grace by faith in Jesus.

The only piece of furniture in the Most Holy Place was the ark of the covenant, a chest made of acacia wood covered in gold. It was three and three-quarter feet wide, and two and one-quarter feet deep and high. Poles attached by rings allowed the priests to carry it from place-to-place. Those poles were not removed from the ark until nearly five hundred years later, when the ark was placed in the temple built for God by King Solomon.

Now, perhaps the word ark makes you think of Noah's ark. In Hebrew, the word for Noah's ark means boat, while the word for God's ark means chest. You will see additional names in the Bible for God's holy chest—the ark of the covenant. For example, it is called the ark of the testimony, the ark of God, the holy ark, and the ark of your strength.

Inside the ark of testimony, Hebrews 9:3-4 tells us, sat the tablets of the law which God gave Moses on Mount Sinai. There was also a golden jar filled with manna, the bread from heaven that God's people ate for forty years in the wilderness. Aaron's staff was in there, with almond leaves, flowers, and almonds growing from it. God had used Aaron's staff to miraculously show that he did—indeed—choose Aaron as the High Priest.

How did the contents inside the ark of testimony testify—point—to Jesus? Well, Jesus came to fulfill the law. In Matthew 5:17, Jesus taught, "Do not think that I have come to abolish the Law or the Prophets; I have not come to abolish them but to fulfill them." The prophecies written about Jesus in the Old Testament proved true. Remember the altar for the bread of the presence? Jesus is the Bread of Life. Jesus is also God's choice as our final High Priest. Hebrews 3:1-2 says, "Therefore, holy brothers, you who share in a heavenly calling, consider Jesus, the apostle and high priest of our confession, who was faithful to him who appointed him, just as Moses also was faithful in all God's house."

Now, on top of the ark was a cover—called the mercy seat—beaten out of gold, with two gold cherubim on either side of the cover. The cherubim faced each other, wings stretched over the lid and nearly touching. In a hymn to God, Psalm 80:1b says, "You who are enthroned upon the cherubim, shine forth." God's glory shone from the mercy seat. Did God need to sit on an earthly throne? No, he did not. But, God chose to be with his people in a way that helped them understand he is the King.

What is a cherubim? That's a good question. God created different types of angels. When Adam and Eve sinned, God sent cherubim to guard the gate to the Garden of Eden so no one could enter again. Cherubim also surround the throne of God, ready to do his will. Cherubim are nothing like the greeting

card cherubs you may imagine. They have swords, and they act on God's command to bring justice.

God judges our sin. He also offers us mercy through Jesus. In the days of the Old Testament, the tabernacle sacrifices temporarily cleansed people from the stain of sin. Hebrews 10:3-4 says, "But in these sacrifices there is a reminder of sins every year. For it is impossible for the blood of bulls and goats to take away sins." The sacrifices in the tabernacle were a shadow—or type—that points us toward God's great plan for salvation through Jesus.

The blood of Jesus makes believers sanctified and holy—clean from the stain of sin, and set apart to serve Yahweh. Hebrews 10:10 speaks of Jesus' sacrifice, saying, "And by that will we have been sanctified through the offering of the body of Jesus Christ once for all." Jesus died for us once, and those who believe in him and repent of sin are saved for all eternity.

Where is Jesus now? Hebrews 10:12-14 tells us, "But when Christ had offered for all time a single sacrifice for sins, he sat down at the right hand of God, waiting from that time until his enemies should be made a footstool for his feet. For by a single offering he has perfected for all time those who are being sanctified." Our great High Priest is in the real, heavenly Most Holy Place.

THE DAY OF ATONEMENT

Ten days after the Feast of Trumpets reminded people of God's coming judgment, the Day of Atonement reminded them of God's salvation plan.

The High Priest purified himself and carried a censer of incense into the Most Holy Place. After sprinkling the blood of a bull on the front of the mercy seat to atone for his own sins, the High Priest sprinkled a goat's blood, atoning for the sins of the Israelites. A second goat was symbolically given the sins of the people, then driven away from Israel.

Today, Jesus' sacrifice on the cross made a way for each of us to be reconciled to God. To be forgiven for

all eternity, you must believe in Jesus, confess him with your mouth, and repent.

WE WORSHIP
GOD'S WAY

On the last evening before Jesus' death, Jews from across the Roman Empire journeyed to Jerusalem to sacrifice their precious Passover lambs as payment for their sins. Jesus and the disciples ate their Passover meal in the upper room of a generous man's house. That's when Jesus instituted or established the Lord's Supper, also called Communion.

Jesus blessed the bread, saying, "Take; this is my body." Next, Jesus thanked God the Father for a cup of wine, sharing it so that everyone drank from the same cup. He said, "This is the blood of the covenant, which is poured out for many." This was a new feast that Jesus, who is God the Son, gave us to remember his sacrifice for us.

Jesus and his disciples sang a hymn, then went to pray at the Mount of Olives, where Jesus was arrested. Though Jesus never sinned, he was crucified the next day. As he hung on the cross, the Lamb of God sacrificed for the sin of the world, God made the land completely dark, right in the middle of the day—from noon until three in the afternoon. Jesus cried out, "My God, my God, why have you forsaken me?"

Then, he died. With Jesus' last breath, the temple veil into the Most Holy Place tore from the top right down to the bottom. Jesus was placed in a tomb on Friday evening, and on Sunday morning he rose from the dead.

Today, we are under a New Covenant with God. Though we no longer worship in the tabernacle or sacrifice animals to cover our sin, we still must worship God in God's way. Hebrews 12:28b says, "Let us offer to God acceptable worship, with reverence and awe." Throughout Scripture, God's people gathered to read the Word of God and to pray. Those aspects of worshiping God have not changed since the time of Moses.

Just as the book of Hebrews has much to say about how the tabernacle pointed to Jesus, it also says much about how we ought to worship God acceptably—in God's way. Jesus is the Lamb of God who died for the sins of all who follow him. His once-and-for-all sacrifice cleansed all believers of their sin. Hebrews chapter 10 tells us the veil is ripped open. Now we can enter the holy places—we can approach God, clean of the stain of sin, because of the blood of Jesus. Because of this, we should not purposefully continue to sin. If we do, it is like trampling the Son of God under our feet. That is a terrible offense.

Just as Jesus and his followers sang a hymn to the Father, Hebrews 2:12 and 13:15 tells us to acknowledge God's name and sing praise to our God. Our praise is a sacrifice we offer to the Lord. The book of Psalms is a book of hymns. It contains praise songs, laments—sad songs when life is hard, songs of thanksgiving, calls for judgment, and even prophecies that point to Jesus. The apostle Paul tells us to sing psalms, hymns, and spiritual songs. We are to sing to God!

Did you know that serving others is a part of worshiping God in an acceptable way? It's true! The

people in God's family are a part of the body of Christ and we are called to care for each other. Hebrews chapter 13 teaches us that there are even more sacrifices that are pleasing to God. For instance, we should show love to our brothers and sisters in Christ. We must offer hospitality to strangers—bringing them into our homes, feeding them, and telling them how to be saved by Jesus.

There's more. Hebrews 13 also instructs us to remember believers in prison and Christians who

are mistreated. How can we care for persecuted Christians? We can pray for them, give money to meet their needs, send Bibles, and even visit them.

We're not done yet! We are to honor marriage— it is an important institution that God gave us in the Garden of Eden. Also, we must honor God's teachings and the leaders of his church. Their job leading us should be a joy, not a misery.

Hebrews 13 has even more to say about worshiping God his way. We should be content with what God has given us, not loving money. Not only that, we ought to do good by sharing what we have. When we give to others in need, that is a sacrifice that pleases God.

Christians are a part of God's church throughout time, and Jesus is the founder and perfecter of our faith. As we worship our holy God, let's offer acceptable worship, remembering that God is with us—both at church, and in our homes. Remember, John 1:14 says, "And the Word became flesh and dwelt among us, and we have seen his glory, glory as of the only Son from the Father, full of grace and truth." Anywhere we go, the God of the Universe goes with us.

THE FEAST OF TABERNACLES

For forty years, the Israelites lived in tents in the wilderness, following God's presence in the pillar of cloud and fire. To remind the people that the Lord dwelled among them, God instituted or established the Feast of Tabernacles.

Following the fruit harvest, everyone traveled to Jerusalem. There, families built small booths and

covered them with palm branches, myrtle and citron boughs, and willow limbs. The little tents must have smelled wonderful! For eight days, families offered sacrifices and feasted before the Lord. It was a joyful time of giving thanks.

As we read the story of Moses, the Exodus, and the tabernacle in God's Word, we remember that Yahweh has always been with his people. He is with us. Praise God for his great plan for our salvation!

TIMELINE

Note: The dating for the rule of Pharaohs in Ancient Egypt varies, as calendars varied. Also, there are two widely accepted dates for the Exodus. This timeline is based on the early date. The early date of the Exodus works backward from dates in Scripture, and is supported by many conservative scholars. Today, biblical scholars are still not entirely certain who the Pharaoh of the Exodus is.

c. 3000 BC

Upper and Lower Egypt unite, and Memphis is built on the boundary of the two to unite Egypt. The city was the capital of the Old Kingdom.

c. 2630 BC

The first pyramid, the Step Pyramid, is built in Saqqara, Egypt by Pharaoh Djoser. It takes twenty years to build.

c. 2560 BC

Pharaoh Khufu builds the Great Pyramid in Giza, Egypt. Originally 755 feet tall (now 481 feet), it is considered one of the Seven Wonders of the Ancient World—and the only one that still exists.

2166-1991 BC

The life of Abraham. God's covenant with Abraham establishes the Israelites as his chosen people.

2066 BC

Isaac, Abraham's son is born.

2006 BC

Jacob, Isaac's son, is born right after his twin brother, Esau. God later renames Jacob Israel. Jacob becomes the father of the twelve tribes of the nation of Israel.

c. 1971 BC

The Temple of Amun, the Egyptian false god of the sun, is built by Pharaoh Senusret I in Karnak, Egypt. The Karnak Temple Complex is used daily for over 1,700 years.

1915 BC

Joseph is born to Jacob and his wife, Rachel.

1886 BC

Isaac dies at 180 years old.

c. 1884 BC

Joseph becomes Egypt's second-in-command after being sold into slavery by his brothers.

c. 1876 BC

Perhaps the date that God brought Jacob's family to Goshen, Egypt, through Joseph.

1859 BC

Jacob dies in Goshen, after seventeen years in Egypt. He is 147 years old when he dies.

1805 BC

Joseph dies in Egypt at 110 years old. Joseph makes his brothers swear they will take his bones with them when God leads them out of Egypt.

c. 1750 BC

King Hammurabi rules Babylon and writes the Code of Hammurabi, 282 laws carved in stone. Moses would have studied this law code during his education in Egypt.

1570-1293 BC

The 18th Dynasty of Egypt is the strongest period of rule for Ancient Egypt.

1595 BC

The Hittites defeat Babylon.

c. 1570-1070 BC

The New Kingdom in Egypt. Thebes (now called Luxor) was the capitol of Egypt at the time. The temples of Luxor and Karnak were located in the city, with the Valley of the Kings burial ground just three miles outside the city.

1526 BC

Moses is born. His mother hides him in a basket in the Nile where the Pharaoh's daughter bathes. Pharaoh's daughter adopts Moses.

1504-1453 BC

Pharaoh Thutmose III reigns over Egypt. A tomb painting for his prime minister, Rehkmire, shows foreigners making bricks. Thutmose III expands his empire into Canaan.

1504-1483 BC

Hatshepsut rules as the only female Pharaoh. Some people think Hatshepsut may have been Moses' adoptive mother.

c. 1453-1425 BC

Pharaoh Amenhotep II reigns over Egypt. The early date for the Exodus would indicate that Amenhotep II was the Pharaoh of the Exodus. Scripture does not indicate that Pharaoh followed his army into the Red Sea.

1486 BC

Moses kills the Egyptian overseer at age 40. He flees Egypt and spends forty years as a shepherd in Midian.

c. 1450-1027 BC

The Shang Dynasty rules in China.

1446 BC

The Exodus happens, and Moses is eighty years old! The Israelites celebrate the first Passover and leave captivity in Egypt. This is the early date for the Exodus.

- The people bring the bones of Joseph out of Egypt with them.

- God gives instructions for the tabernacle and the Israelites construct the portable temple.

1446-1445 BC

The Israelites camp at Mount Sinai, where God gives them the Law. They make and worship the golden calf, sinning terribly.

1446-1406 BC

The Israelites remain in the wilderness.

1406 BC

Moses dies at 120 years of age. Joshua leads the Israelites as they begin their conquest of Canaan.

c. 1208 BC

Pharaoh Merneptah inscribes an account of his victory over ancient Libyans in stone. The Merneptah Stele mentions a battle against Israel in Canaan around 1230 BC. It is the oldest mention of Israel in writing that we have, outside of the Bible.

c. 1200 BC

The Hittite Empire collapses. The Hittites had controlled a huge territory, from Turkey, to parts of Syria and Lebanon.

c. 1164 BC

Egypt loses much of its power in the ancient world.

c. 966 BC

The Israelite Temple is finished and dedicated, built under Solomon, 480 years after the Exodus (1 Kings 6:1).

c. AD 30

Jesus is crucified. He is raised from the dead and ascends to heaven.

WORKS CONSULTED

Blaylock, Richard. "The Doctrine of Reprobation." The Gospel Coalition. https://www.thegospelcoalition.org/essay/doctrine-of-reprobation/. Accessed October 2022.

Boice, James Montgomery. *The Life of Moses: God's First Deliverer of Israel.* P&R Publishing, 2018.

Collins, John. "Miracles." The Gospel Coalition. https://www.thegospelcoalition.org/essay/miracles/. Accessed February 16, 2023.

Currid, John D. and David P. Barrett. *Crossway ESV Bible Atlas.* Crossway, 2010.

"Date of the Exodus." Evidence Unseen. https://www.evidenceunseen.com/date-of-the-exodus/. Accessed October 2022.

Grudem, Wayne. *Systematic Theology: An Introduction to Biblical Doctrine.* Zondervan, 1995.

Hamilton, Adam. *Moses: In the Footsteps of the Reluctant Prophet.* Abingdon Press, 2017.

"How can I achieve victory in Jesus?" Got Questions Ministries. https://www.gotquestions.org/victory-in-Jesus.html. Accessed February 15, 2023.

Janzen, Mark D., Scott Stripling, James K. Hoffmeier, Peter Feinman, Gary A. Rendsburg, and Ronald Hendel. *Five Views on the Exodus: Historicity, Chronology, and Theological Implications.* Zondervan Academic, 2021.

Oliphant, Margaret. *The Atlas of the Ancient World: Charting the Great Civilizations of the Past.* Barnes & Noble Books, 1998.

Packer, J. I. *Knowing God.* InterVarsity Press, 2001.

Pink, Arthur. *The Attributes of God*. The New Christian Classics, 2018.

Rose Book of Bible Charts, Maps & Time Lines. Rose Publishing, 2010.

Rose Guide to the Tabernacle. Rose Publishing, 2016.

Sparks, Bobby L. *The Tabernacle of the Old Testament*. Tabernacle Ministries, 2004.

Sproul, R.C. "What is Providence?" Ligonier. https://www.ligonier.org/learn/articles/what-providence. Accessed February 15, 2023.

The ESV Study Bible™, ESV® Bible. Crossway, 2008.

Tozer, A.W. *The Attributes of God, Volume 1: A Journey into the Father's Heart*. WingSpread Publishers, 2007.

Tozer, A.W. *The Attributes of God, Volume 2: Deeper Into the Father's Heart*. WingSpread Publishers, 2007.

"What is divine providence?" Got Questions Ministries. https://www.gotquestions.org/divine-providence.html. Accessed February 15, 2023.

"What is the Shekinah glory?" Got Questions Ministries. https://www.gotquestions.org/shekinah-glory.html. Accessed February 15, 2023.

Writing for children is a special skill; writing biblical truths for children is a gift! Danika Cooley displays both skill and giftedness in her thoughtful Who, What, Why Series. Engaging, accurate, and compelling, Danika does a beautiful job weaving stories of the Old Testament with Gospel truths found in the New Testament. Thank you, Danika, for pointing children toward Jesus Christ through a better understanding of His Word!

Linda Lacour Hobar
Author of *The Mystery of History*
Chronological, Christian, Complete World
History for All Ages

The Who / What / Why series by Danika Cooley teaches your children more than mere facts about Moses and the Exodus. It teaches them the most important truth we can ever learn in life: Who God is (see John 17:3). As parents and grandparents we can have no greater joy than seeing our children walk in the truth that comes from knowing God. I highly recommend this excellent series.

Israel Wayne
Author, conference speaker,
and founder of FamilyRenewal.org

Books in this series:

Christian Focus Publications publishes books for adults and children under its four main imprints: Christian Focus, CF4K, Mentor and Christian Heritage. Our books reflect our conviction that God's Word is reliable and Jesus is the way to know him, and live for ever with him.

Our children's publication list covers pre-school to early teens. We also publish personal and family devotional titles, biographies and inspirational stories that children will love.

From pre-school board books to teenage apologetics, we have it covered!

Christian Focus Publications Ltd,
Geanies House, Fearn, Ross-shire,
IV20 1TW, Scotland,
United Kingdom.
www.christianfocus.com